THE EUGÉNIE ROCHEROLLE SERIES

Intermediate Piano Solo

Boogie Time

10 Piano Solos arranged by Eugénie Rocherolle

T0195140

ISBN 078 1 5400 0504 6

For all works contained herein:
Unauthorized copying, arranging, adapting, recording, internet posting, public performance,
or other distribution of the music in this publication is an infringement of copyright.
Infringers are liable under the law.

Visit Hal Leonard Online at
www.halleonard.com

Contact us:
Hal Leonard
7777 West Bluemound Road
Milwaukee, WI 53213
Email: info@halleonard.com

In Europe, contact:
Hal Leonard Europe Limited
42 Wigmore Street
Marylebone, London, W1U 2RN
Email: info@halleonardeurope.com

In Australia, contact:
Hal Leonard Australia Pty. Ltd.
4 Lentara Court
Cheltenham, Victoria, 3192 Australia
Email: info@halleonard.com.au

FROM THE ARRANGER

Boogie-woogie has been popular in America since the 1920s. A style of blues piano with lively rhythm, it features a repeated pattern in the bass with melodic variations in the treble. It mostly uses three chords and allows for swing, embellishments, and improvisations. Clarence "Pine Top" Smith (1904-1929) was a popular pianist of boogie style and wrote the first official boogie-woogie song, "Pine-Top's Boogie," in 1928. He was posthumously inducted into the Alabama Hall of Fame in 1991.

I am fortunate to have come of age in an era of cool boogies and swing. I learned to play boogie at a young age and loved playing by ear and picking out the popular tunes of the day. Some of these are included in this collection, along with a few more recent hits and two original boogies.

A few notes:

BOOGIE ALLA TURCA. This shows how a classical work can stay in its original key and keep the same right-hand melody while being converted to a boogie arrangement,   simply by adding some L.H. boogie patterns!

BOOGIE WOOGIE ROMP and G-WHIZ BOOGIE. I wrote these expressly for this collection. Both use the swing rhythm and the traditional three-chord harmonies with L.H. boogie patterns.

COW-COW BOOGIE. With an easy-going and repetitive L.H., more attention can be given to the R.H. melody, chords, and rhythm. The middle section features a melodic line in unison and contrary motion, before returning to the established rhythmic patterns and harmonies.

ST. LOUIS BLUES. While part of this arrangement is swung, one of the themes lends itself well to a traditional boogie bass in broken octaves.

WHEN THE SAINTS GO MARCHING IN. I treated this arrangement as a theme and variations with the L.H. boogie patterns suggesting ideas for the melodies.

Enjoy!

Eugénie

Eugénie Rocherolle
September 2020

BOOGIE ALLA TURCA

By WOLFGANG AMADEUS MOZART
Arranged by Eugénie Rocherolle

Copyright © 2020 Eugénie Rocherolle
All Rights Reserved   Used by Permission

BOOGIE WOOGIE ROMP

By EUGÉNIE ROCHEROLLE

Copyright © 2020 Eugénie Rocherolle
All Rights Reserved   Used by Permission

COW-COW BOOGIE

Words and Music by DON RAYE,
GENE DE PAUL and BENNY CARTER
Arranged by Eugénie Rocherolle

Copyright © 1941, 1942 UNIVERSAL MUSIC CORP., BEE CEE MUSIC COMPANY and HUB MUSIC COMPANY
Copyright Renewed
This arrangement Copyright © 2020 UNIVERSAL MUSIC CORP., BEE CEE MUSIC COMPANY and HUB MUSIC COMPANY
All Rights Reserved   Used by Permission

13

G-WHIZ BOOGIE

By EUGÉNIE ROCHEROLLE

Copyright © 2020 Eugénie Rocherolle
All Rights Reserved   Used by Permission

HEARTBREAK HOTEL

Words and Music by MAE BOREN AXTON,
TOMMY DURDEN and ELVIS PRESLEY
Arranged by Eugénie Rocherolle

Copyright © 1956 Sony/ATV Music Publishing LLC and Durden Breyer Publishing
Copyright Renewed
This arrangement Copyright © 2020 Sony/ATV Music Publishing LLC and Durden Breyer Publishing
All Rights Administered by Sony/ATV Music Publishing LLC, 424 Church Street, Suite 1200, Nashville, TN 37219
International Copyright Secured   All Rights Reserved

PINE TOP'S BOOGIE

Words by NORMAN GIMBEL
Music by CLARENCE "PINE TOP" SMITH
Arranged by Eugénie Rocherolle

© 1929, 1937, 1955 (Renewed) EDWIN H. MORRIS & COMPANY, A Division of MPL Music Publishing, Inc.
Words Renewed 1983 by NORMAN GIMBEL and Assigned to WORDS WEST LLC (P.O. Box 15187, Beverly Hills, CA 90209 USA)
This arrangement © 2020 EDWIN H. MORRIS & COMPANY, A Division of MPL Music Publishing, Inc. and WORDS WEST LLC (P.O. Box 15187, Beverly Hills, CA 90209 USA)
All Rights Reserved

ST. LOUIS BLUES

Words and Music by W. C. HANDY
Arranged by Eugénie Rocherolle

Copyright © 2020 Eugénie Rocherolle
All Rights Reserved   Used by Permission

WHEN I'M SIXTY-FOUR

Words and Music by JOHN LENNON
and PAUL McCARTNEY
Arranged by Eugénie Rocherolle

Copyright © 1967 Sony/ATV Music Publishing LLC
Copyright Renewed
This arrangement Copyright © 2020 Sony/ATV Music Publishing LLC
All Rights Administered by Sony/ATV Music Publishing LLC, 424 Church Street, Suite 1200, Nashville, TN 37219
International Copyright Secured   All Rights Reserved

WHEN THE SAINTS GO MARCHING IN

Dedicated to my high school alma mater, St. Martin's Episcopal School (Metairie, LA)

Traditional
Arranged by Eugénie Rocherolle

Copyright © 2020 Eugénie Rocherolle
All Rights Reserved   Used by Permission

36

YOU'VE GOT A FRIEND IN ME

from TOY STORY

Music and Lyrics by
RANDY NEWMAN
Arranged by Eugénie Rocherolle

© 1995 Walt Disney Music Company
All Rights Reserved. Used by Permission.

THE EUGÉNIE ROCHEROLLE SERIES

Offering both original compositions and popular arrangements, these stunning collections are ideal for intermediate-level pianists! Many include audio tracks performed by Ms. Rocherolle.

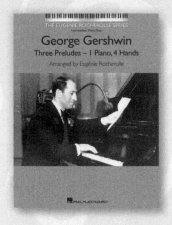

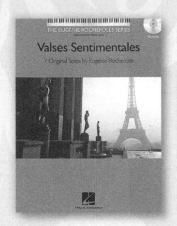

Candlelight Christmas
Eight traditional carols: Away in a Manger • Coventry Carol • Joseph Dearest, Joseph Mine • O Holy Night (duet) • O Little Town of Bethlehem • Silent Night • The Sleep of the Infant Jesus • What Child Is This?
00311808 ....$14.99

Christmas Together
Six piano duet arrangements: Blue Christmas • The Christmas Song (Chestnuts Roasting on an Open Fire) • Rudolph the Red-Nosed Reindeer • Santa Baby • Up on the Housetop • We Wish You a Merry Christmas.
00102838 ....$14.99

Classic Jazz Standards
Ten beloved tunes: Blue Skies • Georgia on My Mind • Isn't It Romantic? • Lazy River • The Nearness of You • On the Sunny Side of the Street • Stardust • Stormy Weather • and more.
00311424 ....$12.99

Continental Suite
Six original piano solos: Belgian Lace • In Old Vienna • La Piazza • Les Avenues De Paris • Oktoberfest • Rondo Capichio.
00312111 ....$12.99

Fantasia del Tango
Six original piano solos (and a bonus piano duet!): Bailando Conmigo • Debajo las Estrellas • Ojos de Coqueta • Promesa de Amor • Suenos de Ti • Suspiros • Tango Caprichoso.
00199978 ....$12.99

George Gershwin – Three Preludes
Accessible for intermediate-level pianists: Allegro ben ritmato e deciso • Andante con moto e poco rubato • Agitato.
00111939 ....$10.99

It's Me, O Lord
Nine traditional spirituals: Deep River • It's Me, O Lord • Nobody Knows De Trouble I See • Swing Low, Sweet Chariot • and more.
00311368 ....$12.99

Mancini Classics
Songs: Baby Elephant Walk • Charade • Days of Wine and Roses • Dear Heart • How Soon • Inspector Clouseau Theme • It Had Better Be Tonight • Moment to Moment • Moon River.
00118878 ....$14.99

Meaningful Moments
Eight memorable pieces: Adagio • Bridal March • Elegy • Recessional • Wedding March • Wedding Processional. Plus, arrangements of beloved favorites Amazing Grace and Ave Maria.
00279100 ....$9.99

New Orleans Sketches
Titles: Big Easy Blues • Bourbon Street Beat • Carnival Capers • Jivin' in Jackson Square • Masquerade! • Rex Parade.
00139675 ....$12.99

On the Jazzy Side
Six original solos. Songs: High Five! • Jubilation! • Prime Time • Small Talk • Small Town Blues • Travelin' Light.
00311982 ....$12.99

HAL•LEONARD®
www.halleonard.com

Prices, contents, and availability subject to change without notice and may vary outside the U.S.A.

Recuerdos Hispanicos
Seven original solos: Brisas Isleñas (Island Breezes) • Dia de Fiesta (Holiday) • Un Amor Quebrado (A Lost Love) • Resonancias de España (Echoes of Spain) • Niña Bonita (Pretty Girl) • Fantasia del Mambo (Mambo Fantasy) • Cuentos del Matador (Tales of the Matador).
00311369 ....$9.99

Rodgers & Hammerstein Selected Favorites
Eight favorites: Climb Ev'ry Mountain • Do-Re-Mi • If I Loved You • Oklahoma • Shall We Dance? • Some Enchanted Evening • There Is Nothin' like a Dame • You'll Never Walk Alone. Includes a CD of Eugénie performing each song.
00311928 ....$14.99

Romantic Stylings
Eight original piano solos: Cafe de Paris • Celebracion • Last Dance • Longings • Memento • Rapsodie • Reflections • Romance.
00312272 ....$14.99

Swingin' the Blues
Six blues originals: Back Street Blues • Big Shot Blues • Easy Walkin' Blues • Hometown Blues • Late Night Blues • Two-Way Blues.
00311445 ....$12.95

Two's Company
Titles: Island Holiday • La Danza • Mood in Blue • Postcript • Whimsical Waltz.
00311883 ....$12.99

Valses Sentimentales
Seven original solos: Bal Masque (Masked Ball) • Jardin de Thé (Tea Garden) • Le Long du Boulevard (Along the Boulevard) • Marché aux Fleurs (Flower Market) • Nuit sans Etoiles (Night Without Stars) • Palais Royale (Royal Palace) • Promenade á Deux (Strolling Together).
00311497 ....$9.99